Meanest Mommy in the Universe

Karen Haywood Queen

D1591063

Library of Congress Control Number: 2022913275

Queen, Karen Haywood.
 Meanest Mommy in the Universe.

ISBN: 978-0-578-81804-7   eISBN: 978-0-578-81805-4
Part memoir and part instruction manual, *Meanest Mommy in the Universe* will make you laugh and inspire you to become a tough parent for the benefit of your entire family.

Dedicated with love to …

Lauren, who kept asking for a book outlining my parenting style.
My children, Ashton and Alyssa, who accompanied me on so many adventures.
My mean parents, Leland and Mary Lee Haywood, who set the mean-with-love standard.
My three siblings, Allen, Laura, and Ibrahim, who always believed in me.
And especially to Eric, my wonderful, mean husband who served in the trenches beside me every day.

Special thanks to early readers Diane Summerville and Alyssa Queen Mitchell; to Terri Fizer, Laura Haywood-Cory, and Sally Benford for editing and project management; and to Ibrahim Peña and Sandy Smith Hernández for website project management.

Cover art by Jorge Nosa. Cover design by Frederic Mitchell III.

Table of Contents

How to Use This Book

If you like to skip around in books as opposed to reading straight through, feel free. Chapters on topics such as mealtime and bedtime are grouped together, but each chapter of *Meanest Mommy in the Universe* stands alone.

At the end of each chapter are action plans for one day, one week, and one month. Follow these plans to strengthen your parenting muscles. On my website, themmitu.com, you can print these plans (password: meanestmommyrocks) to post on your refrigerator to help you stay on track.

Disclaimer: I changed some identifying details but all the stories here are true.

Baby Alyssa completed our family. We posed for a photo on our front porch with our cat, Othello.

Preface: Pushing 'Em Out of the Nest
Why I Wrote This Book and Why You Should Listen to Me

When our son, Ashton, was about 12, I gave him yet another task to do on his own. It might have been the laundry, cleaning the bathroom or perhaps cooking an entire meal (after he washed his hands). He turned to me with suspicious eyes. "You're trying to push me out of the nest, aren't you?"

I told him that my job as a parent was to prepare him to leave the nest.

Here's a checklist of independence goals, many of which I will cover individually in this book. Keep in mind the goal is independence, not necessarily a job well done. Children should learn how to:

- By age 1, sleep through the night.
- By age 3, put their own dishes in the dishwasher.
- By age 4, learn not to whine.
- By age 5, sweep the floor; a bad job is fine.
- By age 5, open a juice box.

- By age 6, serve their own plate with adult supervision.
- By age 6, wipe counters and the kitchen table.
- By age 6, prepare a basic breakfast of cereal and fruit.
- By age 6, prepare a basic lunch at home of sandwiches, chips, and fruit.
- By age 7, pack their lunch for school.
- By age 7, unload and reload a dishwasher with supervision.
- By age 7, dry and put away handwashed dishes.
- By age 10, do their own laundry.
- By age 12, cook several supper dishes and ideally have one signature dish.
- By age 12, do their own daily homework.
- By age 16, apply for jobs and college independently.

Parents, of course, should make exceptions for children with learning disabilities and other special needs.

Becoming the Meanest Mommy in the Universe doesn't mean you don't love your children. Becoming the Meanest Mommy in the Universe will help you transform helpless children into adults who can independently handle life's everyday responsibilities and challenges.

When I started writing this book, my children Ashton and Alyssa were 12 and 8. The *Wall Street Journal*[1] had just reported on a new trend — hyper-involved parents interfering in college students' interactions with professors, administrators, and roommates.

As I finish, Ashton is 29, a civil engineer and a captain in the U.S. Air Force, and a joyful newlywed to Amanda. Alyssa is 25, joyfully married to Frederic Mitchell, and in seminary at Princeton earning dual master's degrees.

The helicopter parent trend is in full swing. Sixty-two percent of parents admitted to completing their child's college application, according to the 2017 *E-Expectations Trend Report*[2]. For some parents, helping complete college applications wasn't enough: The Department of Justice in 2019 charged dozens of high-profile parents in a college admissions scam[3] that involved cheating on exams and lying about students' athletic abilities to get their children accepted to prestigious universities. Some parents said they cheated to show their love for their kids.

Actually, becoming the Meanest Mommy in the Universe is the best way to demonstrate your love for your kids. Why believe me? I'm not the ideal mom, I don't play one on TV nor do I have a doctorate in early childhood education. I do, however, have a bachelor's degree in music education and have taught scores of people to play the piano, including lazy teens, children with special needs, kids that made me laugh, kids that made me cry, kids that other teachers wouldn't teach, kids of Tiger Moms, talented kids, kids lacking in talent, and my own offspring. Mainly, though, I apply the techniques my parents used — raising children with love (often the tough kind), attention (but not too much), support (but never worship), and discipline. As for Ashton and Alyssa, they aren't perfect, but they are good leaders, independent, honest, patient with others, and have fine senses of humor. They know how to cook and do laundry. Both are easy to be around and already making their marks on the world. I am proud of and grateful for them. They are my proof, my bona fides.

Originally, the next two paragraphs featured an even more detailed litany of their successes. Then my friend Diane, an early reader of the book, reminded me that over-managed, over-indulged kids could easily achieve many of these milestones with lots of propping up from parents.

So, I'll do it this way. Unlike many young people, Ashton didn't have a huge adjustment learning about rank, chain of command, and being at the bottom of the totem pole when he joined the U.S. Air Force. He had already experienced those lessons at home. You're welcome, Ashton.

When Alyssa was 20, the 1995 Toyota she drove until 2019 experienced major car-stopping problems with 100 miles to go on a 300-mile trip home to take care of me after my major eye surgery while Eric was at Wallop's Island for a rocket launch. Despite those issues, many parents would have immediately driven 100 miles to solve the problem in person, or at the very least picked up the phone or jumped on the internet to troubleshoot. Not these parents. Instead of relying on us, Alyssa called AAA herself and waited for the tow truck. She called two car repair shops and arranged for the car to be towed to the shop that could make the repair that day.

Kids whose parents act as training wheels throughout high school and into college don't magically become independent after graduating from high school, trade school, or university. At what should be the end of the child-rearing process, you want a child who leaves the nest and sets up their own home. What you don't want is a dependent, entitled 22-year-old child living in your basement. (I realize there are true hardship cases. This is not intended as judgment for the young adults who, especially because of the economy, are temporarily living back home.)

Sadly, that's what happens in many families. More than one-third[4] of adults ages 18-34 live with their parents, according to the U.S. Census Bureau. One that made the news: After five eviction notices didn't do the job, Christina and Mark Rotundo[5] of New York resorted to legal action to push their 30-year-old son out of the nest. He finally moved out in June 2018 after an eight-month process that ended up in court.

Becoming the Meanest Mommy in the Universe is one path to a true empty nest.

In this book, you'll learn why the title of Meanest Mommy or Meanest Daddy in the Universe is a title you want for yourself. I'll give you a plan with action steps to earn that title.

This book works. One early reader began applying the lessons from this book and his preteen daughter evolved from expecting her mom or dad to put her plate and silverware in the dishwasher after meals to cleaning her plate, dumping any remaining crumbs in the trash, and then taking her parents' plates for cleanup. The transformation wasn't just about cleaning plates. Overall, the child became less entitled, more grateful, and a pleasure to have around.

Signs you may need this book:

- When someone asks how you're doing, your response features your child: "Well, I'm busy as usual. Johnny is playing soccer and he has a project due tomorrow."

- You say 'we' when referring to your child, as in "We have to take a driving class," and "We're taking the AP history test next week."
- You call your child a prince or princess and treat him or her as the center of your world. More specifically, you do everything for your tween or teenager including fixing his plate at every meal, washing her clothes, and breaking the budget to produce elaborate birthday extravaganzas.
- When your young adult child has a problem, you step in to troubleshoot every time — calling bosses and professors, registering for classes, and screening roommates. (Colleges have developed apps, social media, and other special programs for such parents.)
- The focus of your family is your child instead of your relationship with your significant other or, if single, your relationship with yourself and other adults.

My friend, Diane, told me, "You are not afraid to take your place in this world. You are not one to be set aside. Placing your children center stage and then falling out of sight was never going to be your parenting style. Yes, that's who you are. It's a good thing. More women should be like you. And it positioned you to be a terrific parent."

A child-centered family is not good for you. Nor is it good for your child.

From the time they were babies, Eric and I knew that eventually, Ashton and Alyssa would be surrounded by people who did not see them as the most important people in the world, or, ahem, the universe. The sooner they realized they were mere tiny specks in a large universe, the better.

Although we never put Ashton and Alyssa on pedestals, we're awed and humbled by being parents. When Ashton was born, Eric and I looked at each other and said, "He needs parents and all he has is … us."

Setting the awe aside, I told Eric I wanted us to raise Ashton so that other people would be happy to babysit him for a weekend or a week for us to get a break. That strategy worked for both kids.

Although the title of this book contains the word 'Mommy,' this book also is for Dads. I advocate that couples work as a team (see page 52). I also keep single parents in mind throughout. As for the word 'Mommy,' I never introduce myself or identify myself as a capital-M Mom except maybe on Mother's Day. I'm a woman who writes about technology and teaches piano. I play music and sing. I kayak, run, hike, travel, and read. I'm active in my church.

Oh yeah, I also happen to have children. See what I did there? I love my children dearly, but they are not the center of my world nor my reason for living.

If your lifelong goal has been to have children and they are in fact the center of your world, good for you. Be happy and fulfilled being a capital-M Mom. But for the sake of those children and the sake of your marriage, keep some of that love, identity, and pride a secret from your children except on their birthdays.

Although the title contains the word 'mean,' I wasn't always mean. Sometimes I was lazy. Often, I was fun. Other times, I was cheap. Although this is not a frugal parenting book, following my suggestions will help you easily save this book's purchase price and more. Watch for this money-saving icon throughout.

Describing someone as mean is not a compliment. So why should you want the title of Meanest Mommy or Meanest Daddy? Perhaps you waited years, endured fertility treatments and/or completed the rigorous adoption process to bring your children home. Your kids are wanted, loved, and special. You want them to have everything you didn't have.

But indulging your children does you no favors. More importantly, indulging your children does *them* no favors. Eventually, your children will emerge into the real world where they aren't special. Better to prepare them now for that day. In telling my story, my goal is to help men and women, who happen to have children, raise their children to become adults who can stand on their own feet.

In case you were wondering, I was voted Meanest Mommy in the World on one of the many days I didn't buy candy or another treat at the grocery store. Then on a day when I refused to carry a teddy bear on a walk around the neighborhood, Alyssa shouted that I was the Meanest Mommy in the *Universe*. About that time, Alyssa also made a note for me. "Wy (why) do you have to by (be) so meen (mean)?" This book answers that question.

----

1. https://www.wsj.com/articles/SB112250452603298007
2. http://learn.ruffalonl.com/rs/395-EOG-977/images/RNL_2017_E_ Expectations%20report_1.0.pdf
3. https://www.justice.gov/usao-ma/pr/arrests-made-nationwide-college- admissions-scam-alleged-exam-cheating-athletic
4. https://www.census.gov/library/stories/2017/08/young-adults.html
5. https://www.npr.org/sections/thetwo-way/2018/06/01/616092288/30-year- old-leaves-the-nest-after-parents-win-court-ordered-eviction

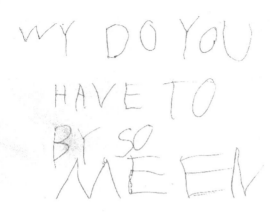

Alyssa wrote this note to me when she was about 5.
I don't remember what I did, but apparently I was meen (mean).

A warm day at Christmas time with Alyssa.
We dressed alike for this picture.

The Meanest Mommy Philosophy

One early reader of the book asked me when, and how, Eric and I developed our parenting philosophy. Honestly, we didn't sit down and come up with a plan. We parent by common sense. Call it a mix of free-range parenting and tough love with no helicopter parenting, no snowplow or tiger mom parenting. I'm writing this parenting book because I've realized that what came naturally to many 1950s and 1960s parents and what came naturally to us does not come naturally to others. This book is your written guide, complete with action plans.

Raise adults, not kids. Many people talk about raising children. Remember, though, our goal is to raise independent adults, not adult-sized children. You'll hear the line about raising independent adults often in this book. When your kids are on their own, they need to be confident in using the tools and performing the tasks of daily living to be self-sufficient. Those tasks include doing laundry, grocery shopping, cooking, managing time wisely, being on time (I'm still working on this one myself), managing finances, and managing their lives in general.

Be their parent, not their friend. I love my kids. I'm not their BFF. If your mom is your BFF, whom do you complain to about your mean mom? Enjoy your children while you have them at home, but don't try to be one of them. You'll look silly and old. Definitely don't try to live through them. You're a separate person.

Never, ever bluff. Kids will call your bluff every time.

R-E-S-P-E-C-T. Treat your kids with respect and expect them to treat you and other adults with respect.

Don't give them more or less autonomy than they can handle. Children should make age-appropriate decisions. Letting kids dictate what's for dinner is age-appropriate only if they bought the food with their own spending money and prepared dinner. As you allow kids to make age-appropriate decisions, empower them to make low-consequences mistakes too. Then by the time they're on their own, they'll be ready to make more serious decisions.

Don't give your power to your children. Use it yourself. Or lose it.

Selfish is not a dirty word. The best moms take time for themselves.

The Most Important Person in the House Is Not Your Kid

Most moms and dads put their adorable babies in the middle of their universe. That's exactly where babies should be. They're cute, helpless, and need constant TLC to survive. The problem is when those babies become toddlers, preschoolers, middle schoolers, high schoolers, and beyond, and remain at the center of mom's and dad's world. These parents strive to please their kids by meeting every need.

Past babyhood, the adults — not the children — are the most important people in the house. When the kids are the most important people in the home, and they know it, chaos reigns.

Here's how the 'most important people in the home' scenario played out after a long day at work for one of my friends. I arrived at her home, meal in hand, at suppertime. My friend is the mother of girls one year apart in age. We'll call them the Almost Twins and her the AT Mom. You'll see the Almost Twins and their mother frequently in this book. AT Mom had just gotten off work and retrieved the Almost Twins from daycare. AT Mom wanted to change clothes, have a drink, and unwind for a few minutes before supper.

Unfortunately, the Almost Twins were wound up, a normal occurrence. Younger Twin was hungry. Instead of telling her to wait, AT Mom offered a cookie. The cookie didn't measure up and Younger Twin threw a fit for cereal (see page 60). AT Mom said, "No cookie," and yelled at Younger Twin. AT Mom then quickly gave in and reached for cereal (see page 63). Older Twin threw a similar tantrum to get her share of attention and her own cookie. AT Mom was verging on a tantrum herself.

I briefly considered a tantrum too. Instead, I stepped into a phone booth and changed into Meanest Mommy in the Universe. I calmly peeled Younger Twin off AT Mom's leg, sent AT Mom to change clothes, told Younger Twin we were eating supper soon, and there would be no cereal. I ignored Younger Twin's full-on pout.

A few minutes later, AT Mom emerged, picked up Younger Twin and asked, "Are you still mad at Mommy?" I was shocked. "*You*," I said, "have nothing to apologize for. You are the Mom. You are the breadwinner and the bread baker. *You* are the most important person in this house. Don't give your power to your children." (See page 78.)

AT Mom smiled at the dawning realization. She does not exist to please and wait on her children. Begging for children's love upsets the natural order and it confuses the kids.

Takeaway: Your needs matter.
Benefit to your kids: They learn patience.
Bonus benefit to you: A calmer home.

Note: Later action plans will include specifics on dealing with whining, demanding, tantrum-throwing children. This action plan is about the big picture idea of recognizing and establishing your importance in the household and recharging your own emotional batteries to better deal with your children.

One-day action plan: If you pick up your children from school or daycare, take five to 30 minutes for yourself first as a transition ritual to get yourself in a parenting frame of mind. Change out of work clothes. Meditate, pray, walk around the block, drink a cup of tea, or an adult beverage. Remind yourself that you're the most important person in your home and the leader of the pack. Brainstorm and list more ideas here:

One-week action plan: Keep doing your transition ritual and reminding yourself of your own importance. Now, create end-of-the-day routines and rituals for your children. Make up a silly song about coming home that you all sing together. When you arrive home, kiss your children the number of times that corresponds with the day of the month — one kiss on the first, two on the second, three on the third, etc. Brainstorm ideas here:

One-month action plan: Set aside 10 to 30 minutes three times a week to nurture the relationship with your spouse, significant other, or another fellow adult. Talk about your day or world events. Take a walk, and if your children are too young to leave home alone, bring them along, but talk to your adult companion. Look back on the month. Chart your progress and the benefits here:

Baby Ashton, child number one, and I were so happy snuggling on the couch. It's OK for babies to be the most important person in the house.

Bedtime with Meanest Mommy
Night and Day, You (Not Your Toddler) Are the One

Ashton, age 3: "I'm going to stay up all night and play with my cars."

We still laugh when recalling that remark. By the way, if he did stay up that night, the all-nighter didn't involve us.

When you have babies, sleep-deprived nights are a given. Parents are programmed to respond to an infant's piercing cries. Good parents must let babies' needs take priority.

As your child matures past babyhood, however, night-time interruptions should no longer be a regular thing. Kids need to go to bed at a reasonable hour so they'll get enough sleep. Just as important, kids need to go to bed at a reasonable hour so their parents can have some downtime.

By 8 p.m., Ashton and Alyssa needed to be finished with that last drink of water and be down for the night in their own beds, preferably, but not necessarily, sleeping. We said, "Go to bed," and that's what happened. We didn't say, "Go to sleep." They were free to stay awake as long as they stayed in bed.

Unless they are sick or fighting monsters in nightmares, kids also need to stay in bed and not wake up their parents. To succeed, you must maintain your meanness. For a few nights, you may sleep even less. The reward will be good sleep in the long term.

When Ashton or Alyssa woke up scared, sick, or in pain, one of us (not always the mom) went to the child's room where we loved them, reassured them, and then returned to the master bedroom without the kids in tow. I'll say that again: without the kids in tow. Often, we even locked our bedroom door at night. In fact, that's how we upgraded from one child to two.

That brings me to another point: co-sleeping. Our kids never slept with us — not all night, not even for part of the night. If co-sleeping works for you, great. I hear you when you talk about the big happy family bed, the joy of snuggling all night long. I am not opposed to co-sleeping if that's what the parents really want.

I am, however, baffled by parents, such as the AT Mom, who don't like co-sleeping, but put up with children in their beds anyway. I listen, mystified, as these parents explain/complain they can't sleep because their children — sometimes age 12 and beyond — wake their parents up to climb into their bed almost every night.

If you know you can't sleep with a squirming baby, toddler, child, or (gasp) preteen sharing your bed, don't start. If you've already started and co-sleeping doesn't work for you, stop it. Tell your night-wandering children it's time to sleep through the night in their own beds. When they cry, comfort them and return to your bed. Each time they cry, let them wait a little longer before you respond. Eventually, your children will soothe themselves back to sleep.

Takeaway: Kids need to learn they are separate people from their parents. One way to learn that lesson is to stay in their own beds, unless parents have actively chosen co-sleeping.
Benefit to your kids: More independence.
Bonus benefit to you: More independence. More sleep.

One-day action plan: If your children wake up in the night crying, go to them, hug them, reassure them of your love, and then return to your own bed without kids in tow. If your children cry, wait five minutes before going back into their rooms. If the kids come to your bed, walk them back to their own rooms. Chart your progress here:

One-week action plan: Repeat the one-day action plan and add five minutes of crying time each night. Brace yourself for loud crying. Be strong. Remember, eventually your children will give up and go back to sleep on their own. Chart your progress here:

One-month action plan: Continue the one-week action plan. By now, your children should have gotten the message. Remember, don't give in even for one night or you'll have to start all over. Chart your progress here:

Ashton picking a bouquet for me.

Bedtime with Meanest Mommy
Getting Up in the Morning Starts the Night Before

The Almost Twins fight going to bed almost every night. AT Mom turned to me in desperation because one of the Almost Twins also refused to get up in the morning. No surprise since she wasn't getting enough sleep. They were late for school almost every day.

I advised, "Tell Almost Twin she has to go to bed an hour earlier tonight because she didn't get up this morning." AT Mom responded, "I told her that and she hated it." I replied, "That is the point. She's not supposed to like it."

Then I backed up. That early bedtime as punishment might work with many kids. However, Almost Twin is a strong-willed, stubborn child. So, instead of framing an early bedtime as a punishment, I suggested AT Mom frame her message to her daughter as assistance. "Tell her you're trying to *help* her. Tell her that to help her get up earlier like she's supposed to, she needs to go to bed earlier."

The first night, Almost Twin tried to start a different battle by refusing to take a shower. AT Mom refused to fight head-on or to play that game. Instead, AT Mom responded, "Fine, no shower tonight. You're still going to bed. Remember, this is helping you."

Stubborn Twin went to bed. From the pillow she said, "I think I'll go to bed early every night so I can do better at school." The next day, she got up on time.

Takeaway: Smooth mornings begin with a consistent, early bedtime.
Bonus takeaway: At bedtime and beyond, you don't have to fight every battle directly to win.
Benefit to your kids: More sleep.
Bonus benefit to you: More sleep. Smoother mornings.

One-day action plan: If your children have trouble getting up in the morning, tell them you're on their side. You're going to help them get up by having them go to bed earlier. Take away all electronics at least an hour before bedtime. Remind your children that you are helping them, not punishing them. Chart your progress here:

One-week action plan: Tell your children that any day they don't get up on time in the morning, you'll know they aren't going to bed early enough. To help them, bedtime will become even earlier that night. Don't get mad. Just plainly state the consequences — ahem, the help — you'll provide. Chart your progress here:

One-month action plan: Tell your children that for every week they get up on time every day, they can stay up 30 minutes later on a weekend night. Chart your progress here:

Bonus action plan: Keep track of the battles you've won by not fighting them head on. Chart your progress here:

Mornings with Meanest Mommy

Getting Up in the Morning:
Not a Parent Problem

One early reader of this book took the lessons to heart. His preteen daughter wasn't keen on getting up in the morning. Dad had to repeatedly wake, shake, and re-wake the kid to get her up, so Dad could drive his kid to school and the kid could arrive on time.

One morning when the girl wouldn't get up, Dad didn't get up either. He just rolled back over. After a few minutes, the daughter realized that Dad was still snoozing. Daughter got up. Daughter fixed her breakfast and packed her lunch — tasks she didn't usually do for herself. Daughter gathered her books and lunch, and said she was ready. Daughter was now worried they'd be late. The burden of being on time already was shifting from Dad to daughter.

Finally, Dad slowly, leisurely got out of bed and walked to the car where daughter was waiting. Dad got in the car, sat down, and buckled up. Then he unbuckled. "Oh wait, I forgot something." Dad went back into the house. By now, daughter was truly worried. Dad asked, "What happens at school if you're late?" Daughter didn't know. Dad told daughter, "You may find out today. You're the one going to school, not me." Daughter sweated all the way to school. They arrived at school on time. Daughter apologized to Dad.

At pickup time, daughter apologized again. Daughter is a lot more likely to get up and get ready now. All Dad has to do is yawn and head back toward bed.

Takeaway: In general, don't let your children's problems become your problems. Specifically, be willing to let your child face the consequences for being late for school and other activities.
Benefit to your kids: They become punctual and self-sufficient.
Bonus benefit to you: You worry only about problems that are truly yours.

One-day action plan: Tell your child that getting up in the morning is his problem, not yours. If both parents work outside the home, arrange for one of you to work from home that morning or come in a little late, if possible, so that you can truly not care about being late yourself. If your child refuses to get up, head back to bed or head to your computer to start work. If your child misses the bus, take 'cab fare' out of his allowance. Chart your progress here:

One-week action plan: Buy your child an old-fashioned alarm clock (also useful for when you have to take her cell phone away). Show her how to use the alarm clock. Tell her that you're no longer providing a wake-up service. Repeat the one-day action plan as often as needed. Let your child's teacher know what is going on and that you're happy for your child to face consequences at school for missed class time. Tell your child that in addition to consequences at school, consequences for tardiness will include losing her cell phone. Chart your progress here:

One-month action plan: Expand the idea beyond school to other activities and events that your child must be on time for. If your child is not ready to leave at the time you set, then don't go. Chart your progress here:

Mornings with Meanest Mommy
Whose Lunch Is It Anyway?

Many of my friends get up early, prepare a hot breakfast, serve it to their children, take their children's plates, dump leftover food in the trash (see page 92), then wash those plates. Next, the parents fix lunches for their children, even their teenagers.

Although I'm a morning person, I didn't always get up with my preteen and teen kids. Sometimes, if I hadn't slept well, I was still in bed when Ashton and Alyssa got up. On those days, they prepared and ate breakfast, fixed their lunches, and caught the bus on their own with no adult hovering. Meanest Daddy, a night owl, often was still asleep as well.

Some mornings when I did get up early, I said "Good morning" to Ashton and Alyssa and then went running. Yes, I left the house and went running while my middle and high school kids were getting themselves ready for school. On other days, I walked to the bus stop with Ashton or Alyssa, talked about their lives and mine, then continued on my walk or run after they got on the bus. They were particularly embarrassed by the reflector vest I wore on dark mornings.

Because I wasn't on hand every day, Ashton and Alyssa appreciated me on the mornings I spent with them. Even when I was around, most days Ashton and Alyssa still fixed their own breakfast and school lunches. When they were in a rush, they asked for my help with breakfast and/or lunch. They didn't expect it. Often, they even said thank you.

Diane has three kids compared to my two, and thus she has had more opportunity to perfect her mean-mommy philosophy. Sometimes when Diane was in a rush, her youngest child helped her fix her breakfast and lunch. I'm in awe.

Takeaway: Teach independence one breakfast and one lunch at a time.

Benefit to your kids: On a practical level, they learn to put together breakfast and lunch on their own without your hovering or help. On a philosophical level, they learn that the world, and their parents' lives, don't revolve around them.

Bonus benefit to you: A morning run or walk, or a little extra sleep.

One-day action plan: If you've been trying unsuccessfully to add a morning walk, run or bike ride, yoga, meditation, or a cup of coffee or tea alone to your morning routine, add it tomorrow morning. If your children are 6 and older, tell them the night before that they can be grown up in the morning and prepare their own breakfast and lunch. Give suggestions and show them what they'll need. Chart your progress here:

One-week action plan: Set a goal of two weekday plus one weekend sessions of you-time while your children prepare their own breakfasts and lunches. The other days, stay home and be available for them. Remind your children to be grateful and that your help is not always a given. Chart your progress here:

One-month action plan: Increase your you-time activity by one day. On school holidays and breaks, invite your children to enter your world and go along with you on a walk or run once a week. Chart your progress here:

Don't Waste Time by Delaying Potty Training

You might want to swallow your drink before reading further. As much as I'd like to maintain an author's authoritative air of always being right, sometimes I make mistakes. Spring and summer are supposed to be good times for toilet training because you can let the kid run around with no pants on.

Not potty training Ashton the summer he turned 2 was a major error on my part.

My friend Elle's son is only three days older than Ashton. The summer the boys turned 2, Elle told her son that they'd run out of diapers and he had to start using the potty. In contrast, I wasted (pun intended) that summer and allowed Ashton to wear diapers until the following summer when he turned 3. At $8 a box of diapers and one box per week, I wasted more than $400 that year on … waste, and wasted a lot of time changing diapers.

The following summer, we finally got the job done. Overall things came out fine. Except for this incident.

When Elle's son and Ashton were about 4, the boys spent the afternoon playing at our house. Elle's son wanted to show off and did #1 in the yard. Ashton, ahem, one-upped his friend and did #2. On the front porch.

Takeaway: Using the bathroom alone is a key maturity milestone for toddlers. Make time to help your child ditch the diapers and achieve that milestone. Start toilet training early.
Benefit to your kids: The independence and pride of learning a key life skill.
Bonus benefit to you: No more changing diapers. More, ahem, disposable income.

One-day action plan: If your child is 2 or 3 or (yikes) 4 and not yet potty trained for daytime, start today. Buy a kiddie potty. Put away the diapers. Buy some training pants and some treats. Chart your progress here:

One-week action plan: Tell your child the diapers are gone. Show him the new potty and tell him and it's time to pee in that potty. Help him put on his new big-boy training pants. Give him lots of water. Show him the treats he'll get when he pees in the potty. Remember, there will be setbacks. Don't judge or shame your child when he has an accident. Just get fresh training pants and sit him on the potty again. Chart your child's progress here:

One-month action plan: If your child has made it through most of the month going to the potty during the day, consider starting night-time potty training. Use two pairs of training pants at night and put a plastic sheet under the regular sheet. Some children are sound sleepers and night potty training takes a while. If your child can't make it through the night or doesn't wake up to go, then you have my permission to use diapers or Pull-Ups.® Even if you're using diapers at night, you're still saving money and your child has still reached a maturity milestone. Chart your progress and add up the savings here:

I Hate You, Mommy

I was eating dinner with the AT mom and the Almost Twins. Out of the blue, the AT mom asked her oldest daughter: "Why are you mad at Mommy?" Nothing had happened. My friend was reading the frown on her daughter's face as anger directed at her.

First, sometimes a frown is simply … a frown. Second, that type of question encourages passive-aggressive behavior but that's the topic of another book. Third, if the mom had in fact applied serious consequences or discipline, the result might well be a frown with no apology needed.

Takeaway: If you aspire to the mean mommy ranks, you can't take your children's frowns and comments personally. You'll get called ugly and mean (see page 19). They'll tell you they hate you. You'll get called, yes, the Meanest Mommy in the Universe.

One-day action plan: The next time your child says he hates you or calls you mean and/or ugly, blithely respond: "OK." Then continue with your day. Chart your progress here:

One-week action plan: If you constantly ask your child if she is doing OK based on her facial expression, stop. Chart your progress here:

One-month action plan: If your child goes into a lengthy pouting session and you worry something terrible may be wrong, let him pout for at least an hour before asking. Chart your progress here:

Meanest Parent Rules

When is the Meanest Mommy in the Universe not the meanest parent in the Universe? When Daddy or Mama is even meaner (Here is where we acknowledge different kinds of households: one mom, one dad, two moms, two dads, grandparents, aunts, uncles, guardians.) The point is, kids should not be allowed to shop among the adults in their lives for the best answer. Eric and I have a saying in our house: "Meanest parent rules." In practice, that has meant the kids can't parent-shop to see which one of us will give the best answer to, "Can I please wear black eyeliner just this once?" Or, "Everyone else is staying out all night at the bonfire on the beach — can I stay too?" Or, "Can I get a car when I'm 16?"

When parent-shopping isn't allowed, there's no "But Daddy/Mommy said" comeback from the kids because they know the drill. Whichever parent is the strictest or most worried has veto power, or "Meanest parent rules." End of discussion.

For example, the kids had to wear life jackets swimming in the ocean until: A) They turned 10 and B) I was confident they were strong swimmers. Ashton and Alyssa wore life jackets (see page 136) and I didn't have to worry as much about death by drowning. Alyssa is still recovering from the indignity of wearing a life jacket the summer Ashton was allowed to ditch his life jacket.

Even though Eric thought my life jacket stance was too strict, he never pushed me. I didn't have to convince anyone I was right. I knew that I had the final word if I wanted it. Same for Mean Daddy when he was strict.

Does Meanest Parent Rules mean the Meanest Parent never backs down? Of course not. I've backed down from a strict position after giving it more thought. The life jacket issue was one example. The next summer, Alyssa demonstrated she was a strong swimmer and she got to give up her life jacket, too, even though she was only 7 at the time.

Takeaway: Parenting is a team sport. This rule is even more important for parents not living together. Present a united front. If you're a single parent, you still need to present a united front by not waffling on your positions (see page 63).
Benefit to your kids: They realize they can't parent-shop for the best answer.

Bonus benefit to you: No parent-shopping. A stronger marriage — or a friendlier divorce. Possible money savings on items ranging from makeup to Mazdas.

One-day action plan: Talk to your spouse, co-parent, or even yourself about this rule and what it would mean to your relationships with each other and your children. Brainstorm ideas here:

One-week action plan: Implement the "Meanest parent rules" rule (whatever the strictest parent says, goes, and no parent-shopping) with your children. Explain what it means so there are no misunderstandings. Repeat the process every time a new issue arises. Chart your progress here:

One-month action plan: Talk to your spouse, co-parent, or yourself about how the rule is going. List the benefits here:

Count up the financial savings and list them here:

Having a blast at Surfside Beach, S.C.
Not pictured: life jackets.

I Don't Speak Whine

"Moooooommeee, heeeeeeee hiiiiit meeeeee. Moooooommeee, my foooooooot hurts. Moooooommee, I don't liiiiiiike carrots."

Just reading that sing-song whine gets on your nerves, doesn't it?

Nature or nurture? I don't know whether children are born knowing that special voice or whether how to whine is a sacred secret passed down every year from confident kindergarteners to their preschool protégées.

When kids whine, they're looking for attention. If they don't get attention, there's no reason to whine.

About the tenth time Ashton, as a newly-minted preschooler, tried out whining, I'd had enough. I looked him in the eye and responded, "I don't understand whine." Blank look. "I can't hear you when you're whining. Say it without whining." After a few tries, Ashton got his message across in a normal voice.

That conversation didn't end whining forever in our house. But every instance of whining got that response. That is, no response to whatever the whiner was saying until he or she could speak in a normal, not-whining tone of voice.

Back to the big picture: Once the No Whining Revolution is won, the 5-year-olds can teach the 4-year-olds a more useful skill — maybe blowing their noses without help.

Takeaway: Don't respond to whining. If you ignore whining every time, your children will stop.
Benefit to your kids: They learn that not only do words matter, so does tone of voice.
Bonus benefit to you: No whiiiiiiiiiiining.

One-day action plan: The next time your child whines, either ignore him or look him in the eye and say, "I can't hear you when you whine. Use your normal voice." Chart your progress here:

One-week action plan: Track how many times your child whines and how many times you respond, "I can't hear you when you whine. Use your normal voice." Chart how many times your child changes their voice and how many times they just walk away. Chart your progress here:

One-month action plan: Try this technique on your children's playmates. Chart your progress here:

The (Only) Temper Tantrum

The younger Almost Twin is always working herself into a state over something she wants. Sometimes that state lasts for hours and involves hyperventilating and using her inhaler.

Kids do whatever gets results. Almost Twin's tantrums bring results. Often, she gets what she wants even if the original answer was no (see page 63). Other times, Almost Twin doesn't get what she's asking for, but she still gets something valuable to her — adult attention.

Don't play the game. Don't feed the beast. The goal is to care about the kid, but not about the tantrum.

Here's how Ashton's temper tantrum worked out: Ashton, 4, and I were in the kitchen. He wanted something. Whatever it was, I wasn't giving it to him. Ashton threw himself on the floor for his first-ever temper tantrum. He pounded his fists. He kicked his feet. He screamed. He looked at me out of the corner of his eye.

I said, "Is that all you got? I've seen 2-year-olds throw better temper tantrums."

Ashton looked confused. This was not the response his preschool friends told him he'd get. Finally, seeing that I wasn't moved by his performance, Ashton gave up and got up. His first temper tantrum became his last.

Because of that non-reaction on my part, we never had to deal with temper tantrums at home, in the grocery store or elsewhere. As with whining, reacting to a child's tantrum feeds the beast that produces the tantrum.

Takeaway: On the surface the tantrum is about getting candy, avoiding a nap, or in general, getting his own way. However, the child's real goal is getting attention — either positive or negative. Your indifference is a better reaction than either hugs or anger. **Benefit to your kids:** They learn how the real world works. **Bonus benefit to you:** You don't have to endure multiple tantrums, fits, and pouting spells.

One-day action plan: The next time your child has a temper tantrum, ignore the tantrum and ignore your child. Don't give in. Don't yell. Just read a book, especially this book. Chart your progress here:

One-week action plan: When your child has a tantrum, tell her that tantrums are for babies. Children hate being compared to babies. Repeat the one-day action plan as needed. Chart your progress here:

One-month action plan: Look back over the month. If you gave in to a tantrum, note what else was going on with you or with your child. Consider what you could do to prevent that situation next time. Chart your progress here:

We Don't Negotiate with Terrorists:
No Means No

Two years had passed. Ashton, age 6, wanted something yet again. Kids are always wanting something! Eric said no. Ashton already knew a temper tantrum wouldn't work (see page 60). He also knew parent-shopping wouldn't work (see page 52).

Instead, Ashton tried to broker a deal to change 'no' to 'yes.'

Eric responded, "We don't negotiate with terrorists." Our friend Dave thought that was hilarious.

When they want something, which is nearly all the time, children are like terrorists. They see only their viewpoint and the rest of the world doesn't matter.

I hear you: You want to make the whining and pleading stop. Giving the kid what he wants shuts the kid up and makes the next 15 minutes much better. But you kick the whining can down the road (see page 57).

You buy peace for the next 15 minutes at the expense of peace of mind for the next 15 years.

As a mean, lazy, selfish mom, I have been a strong believer in saying 'no' consistently. Two-year-olds want more candy. Twelve-year-olds want more computer time and more candy. Sixteen-year-olds want a later curfew, more screen time, and more candy.

Until I started coaching the mother of the Almost Twins, her most frequent response to every question also was 'no.' You might think that as Meanest Mommy in the Universe, I'd praise that response as good parenting.

Actually, I would not. There's a difference between a consistent 'no' and a 'no' that is only the first step on a long, painfully negotiated road to 'yes.' Even worse than saying 'yes' every time is saying 'no' at first, and then later giving in to the negotiating and constant pleading, and switching that initial 'no' to 'yes.'

When AT mom says 'no,' the Almost Twins wear her down quicker than they can gobble a handful of potato chips. She dreams of a calm house, but until AT Mom can make her 'no' stick, her house will continue to be a house of chaos.

Children are optimists. If you have backed down from 'no,' even once, your kid hopes you'll back down again. With even a one percent chance of, "No, we aren't buying that toy or candy" converting to a resigned "Yes, you can have the thing," kids are going to go all-in on whining and negotiating. Every time you say 'no,' you'll experience whining, wheedling, arguing, negotiating, and full-blown tantrums.

Most times, consistency is more important than the so-called right answer. If you constantly change 'no' to 'yes,' you'd be better off saying 'yes' in the first place.

Sometimes 'no' isn't the right answer. Sometimes you should just skip that long and winding road and go straight to 'yes' when your child makes a request. Can we have eggs for supper? Yes. Can we go on a walk? Let's go! Will you listen to me play my song? Yes indeed. Can I play outside? Sure! Can I climb in your lap? Yes!

Look for reasons and ways to say 'yes.' Those yeses are money in the bank for when you must say 'no.'

Finally, never enter a battle you can't win. When you get overwhelmed with whining, or other behavior, don't answer right away. Tell your children you need to think about the issue and respond later.

Changing your habits won't be easy at first for you or your kids. But when your children hear 'yes' more often, 'no' won't sting so badly. When kids realize 'no' really does means 'no,' they'll retreat from that battleground.

Takeaway: Just say 'no.' Except when you say 'yes' from the beginning. Once you do say 'no,' don't negotiate.
Benefit to your kids: When the real world says 'no,' they'll recognize the word.
Bonus benefit to you: You won't be plagued with constant kiddie terrorist attacks. You'll enjoy good times with your children from all the times you said 'yes.' You'll have more money in the bank from saying 'no' to candy, toys, and other treats.

One-day action plan: Count to 20 before you give your child an answer to any request. Notice the difference it makes when you take time to think. Chart your progress here:

One-week action plan: When your child asks for something, consider if it's a request you can respond to with 'yes.' If so, cut to the chase and say 'yes.' Chart your progress here:

One-month action plan: When you say 'no,' make it stick. Remember, you've already given the issue some thought and considered if you could respond with 'yes.' Chart your progress here:

Powering Past Interruptions
Meanest Mommy Has a Life

Limiting interruptions is so important that I'm devoting several chapters to the topic.

We've talked about nighttime interruptions (see page 30). Powering past interruptions is also important during the day. I wrote the first draft of this chapter well before the COVID-19 pandemic sent many children home for virtual learning and many of their parents home for remote work. The lessons are trickier, but still apply.

James Taylor did not write his song, *You've Got a Friend*, with its message of, "You just call out my name, and I'll come running" for parents, especially mothers. Adopting an "I'll come running" attitude leads to parents, especially moms, who can't relax at home or focus at work because they are consumed with anticipating and meeting their children's needs.

In the 1950s, many women did stay home along with their children. But they called themselves house*wives*. Their primary focus was on a fellow adult — their husband. They managed their households, volunteered, and, in general, made the world go around. These women also played bridge, met in clubs, gardened, sewed, smoked cigarettes (the first Surgeon General's report on the danger of smoking didn't come out until 1964) and drank coffee (mornings) and martinis (afternoons) while their kids played alone or with each other.

In contrast, many of today's women who have made the choice to stay home and manage their households put their primary focus on tiny tots. Some pour all the energy they spent on earning an MBA and managing a huge marketing or finance team to playing Candy Land with, and micromanaging the lives of, their 2-year-olds, 12-year-olds, and 22-year-olds.

Yes, we've come a long way, baby. Women have more choices than ever. Some lead Fortune 500 companies. Others thrive at homemaking. Losing the cigarettes and daytime martinis were probably good moves for women. But trading an adult-centered world for a child-centered world doesn't do the child or the adult any favors.

As I said, it's trickier when children need adult help to complete actual schoolwork as opposed to mitigating mere boredom. You can, however, help your children work through problems step-by-step before calling out for help (see page 102).

As for boredom, entertaining kids leads to — no surprise — kids who expect to be entertained. That means: whining preschoolers who can't play alone noisily or quietly; children and tweens who interrupt you while you're chatting with a friend; and teens who expect you to drop everything and come running whenever they call or text. If you occasionally ignore your children, they'll learn to sort out problems and boredom on their own.

Caveat: Yes, I also know Harry Chapin's song, *The Cat's in the Cradle*, with its message of taking time for your children. I'm not advocating that you ignore your child or never play with your child. I am saying your child should be able to entertain herself.

When Ashton was 2 months old, I didn't go back to work at Associated Press. I saved that for the next year. When he was still a baby, I did something far more demanding than returning to the news business: I enrolled part-time in music school for a second bachelor's degree. I had to find time for homework and two hours of piano practice every day.

One day I was practicing Mozart variations when 3-year-old Ashton toddled in with a block. I stopped practicing for just a second and said, "Mommy's playing piano and Ashton... ." He finished, "Better find something to do." He toddled off to play Legos®.

Ashton learned I had a world of my own. He worked to join me in my music-learning, music-playing world. He'd sit at the piano, playing random keys, saying, "major third," and "minor third," imitating me learning musical intervals. He also composed, played and sang a song, "Ice cream is good. I like it too." He learned to play the piano, played bells in the marching band, learned to play bass, and is a good singer, too.

As I write this, Ashton is in his 20s. Would I love to see that toddler with a block again? You bet. Do I regret practicing piano that day and lots of other days? Not a chance. I was working toward a goal, a music degree, and I achieved that goal. Ashton achieved another key goal, independence.

A few nights before I wrote this chapter, I sat down at the piano — yep, that same piano — Ashton pulled out his bass and we spent almost an hour playing and singing rock and jazz tunes. As I put the final editing touches on this book, Ashton was home from Germany for a visit and we sang together at an open mic night.

Takeaway: You live a life separate from your kids. Make that clear.
Benefit to your kids: They learn to be self-sufficient.
Bonus benefit to you: You can achieve your life goals.

One-day action plan: Pick something short to do today that you enjoy. Read for five minutes, drink a cup of tea, or talk to a friend. When your child inevitably interrupts, respond, saying, "I'm reading, drinking tea, talking, practicing music... ." Fill in your own blank. Chart your progress here:

One-week action plan: When your children demand your attention, repeat the response in the one-day action plan and tell your kids, "Come back in five minutes." Every day, increase the number of minutes by one. Give your child some one-on-one time later in the day. Chart your progress here:

One-month action plan: If you work at home, create three signs for your workspace: one red, one yellow, one green. Tell your child they can interrupt you when the green sign is up, can interrupt only for something very important when the yellow sign is up, and only if you need to call 911 when the red sign is up. Also, come up with one to three possible hobbies, volunteer gigs, or career goals to start on. Pick one and begin taking steps toward your own life. Chart your progress here:

Powering Past Interruptions
You're Still the One — Not Your Child

The Almost Twins interrupt their mother constantly. Sometimes she says, "Not now," but her words lack force and confidence (see page 63). The Almost Twins know if they keep pestering, their mother will eventually stop what she's doing and give them attention, even if their need is minor and the immediate problem is one they could solve on their own.

One friend's daughter repeatedly interrupted an adult conversation not because of an emergency, but because she was jealous of her mother talking to someone else.

As a piano teacher, I have worked with many elementary age children who interrupt adults because they can't open juice boxes or use a serving spoon to take food from a serving dish (see page 78).

Kids, especially pampered kids, don't differentiate between major and minor needs. All of their needs are major and immediate.

Actually, the issue of interruptions brings out two traits in play: children interrupting and children not being able to solve problems on their own. Children need to learn not to interrupt adults for every perceived challenge. Kids also must learn how to solve their own problems.

When Ashton and Alyssa were young and I was busy (what parent of young kids isn't busy?!), I told them to carry on without me if their issue didn't involve a fire, gushing blood, or a broken bone sticking out of their skin.

Sometimes I sent them to play outside and locked the doors.

Ashton and Alyssa thought I didn't know they were going to the creek. I knew. The creek wasn't deep enough for them to drown, and I had fond memories of my own childhood playing in our creek.

When Tatum, one of Ashton's favorite playmates, couldn't make it back up the hill from the creek, they didn't interrupt me to come to the rescue. Instead, Ashton found some of his dad's rope, tied the rope to a tree, and helped Tatum summit the muddy hill. Tatum was resourceful, too. Her dear mother had told her not to play in the muddy woods at our house. So, Tatum brought an extra pair of shoes to every playdate.

Meantime, I was writing a story about the coastal Virginia jazz scene, blissfully unaware of the problem-solving, hill-climbing, and life skills-learning taking place a few dozen feet away outside. Like anything else, troubleshooting your own issues is a learned skill. If you want your 20-year-old to be able to handle a car breakdown 100 miles from home (see page 14), start her off with smaller challenges, such as opening her own juice box, making her own sandwich, packing an old pair of shoes for a playdate, and figuring out how to help friends get back up the hill from the creek.

Takeaway: Empower your kids to solve their own problems. Don't allow them to interrupt you for minor issues.
Benefit to your kids: By waiting, they'll develop patience. By trouble-shooting their own problems, they'll develop confidence.
Bonus benefit to you: You'll be able to finish a conversation, a book, and a night's sleep.

One-day action plan: The first time your children interrupt you today, help them break the problem down into small steps. Chart your progress here:

One-week action plan: When your children bring a problem to you to solve, ask them to come up with three ways to solve the issue on their own. Chart your progress here:

One-month action plan: If your children are still constantly interrupting, make interruption tickets. Give your child three tickets per day. For each requested interruption, your child has to give you a ticket. When the tickets are gone, they're gone. Chart your progress here:

Mealtime
Will You *Let* Me Fix You a Plate?

"Will you let me fix you a plate?" Permission Mommy asked her
7-year-old son.

Permission Mommy also has asked her children for permission to
sit beside them at the table, to leave them with a grandparent to go
on a walk, and to allow other adults to play a game with the child.

The first issue is asking the child for permission. Some parents ask
permission without realizing it by how they phrase commands to
their children. "Sit down, OK?" "Eat your supper, OK?" "Put your
plate in the dishwasher, OK?" When parents add "OK?" with the
corresponding vocal uptick, they're not giving their child a
command. Instead, they are giving away their power by implying
that the child can say no to a reasonable request.

I asked Permission Mommy about that power. "He doesn't really
have a choice," she told me. Then why ask permission? Either a
child has the power and the choice or he doesn't. If the son's

choice doesn't stand, then he learns that adults don't keep their word.

Permission Mommy elaborated further. "He doesn't even know what power is." Oh yes, he does. On another occasion, this child demanded to sit at the head of the table during a holiday meal at someone else's home, demonstrating his belief that he outranks the adults in his life.

The other issue is doing things for a child that the child should do for himself. I've seen Permission Mommy and Permission Daddy butter bread for 7-year-olds and cut meat for 13-year-olds.

Keeping your child dependent on you doesn't do your darling any favors. By age 6, your child should be able to serve his plate, open his own juice box (see page 74), and butter his own bread. Make sure the knife is a butter knife, especially if your child is not yet the sharpest knife in the drawer. By age 7, your child should be learning to cut up meat. Parents should supervise to make sure the child cuts meat into bite-sized bits, uses utensils instead of fingers, chooses at least some nutritious food, and doesn't take the last piece of cake (see page 87).

Yes, there will be spills, wasted food, and even broken plates and glasses (see page 89). The messes are worth it, though, to achieve the overall goal: an independent child.

Takeaway: Empower your children by letting them make age-appropriate decisions, such as choosing between wearing the red shirt or the blue shirt to school. Otherwise, don't give away your power. Don't give your child choices inappropriate for his age or position in the family. Further empower your children by enabling them to do tasks for themselves instead of constantly hovering, helping, and doing the tasks for them.

Benefit to your kids: Humility from knowing their rank in the family, and the true confidence that comes from knowing how to do things on their own.

Bonus benefit to you: You keep your power and your rank as an adult in your family.

One-day action plan: Stop asking your child for permission to do favors for him. Chart your progress here:

One-week action plan: At meals, empower your children to fix their own plates, butter their own bread, and cut up their meat. You can still make sure they eat vegetables. Chart your progress here:

One-month action plan: Stop giving your child a choice whether to spend time with another adult. If you're in the habit of adding 'OK?' to your requests, stop that, too. Chart your progress here:

Mealtime
What's for Supper?

Speaking of meals, AT Mom cooked a delicious meatloaf for supper and served it to the Almost Twins. "We don't want meatloaf. We want pizza," they whined (see page 57). So, AT Mom ordered pizza. She threw away a perfectly good meatloaf and spent more money to satisfy ungrateful children.

Although delivery existed back when AT Mom and I were kids, our moms never called out for pizza. If our moms ever had considered pizza delivery, they wouldn't have called out for pizza simply because we turned up our noses at the meal they spent hours cooking. If we had told our moms we didn't like the meal on the table, here are the possible responses:

- Tough. Eat it anyway and don't leave the table 'til you're done.
- Go hungry. Go to bed early.

- A spanking, then eat it anyway, or go hungry. (Note on spanking: This is neither an endorsement nor a condemnation.)

My mean mom forced me to eat lasagna. Cooking lasagna is a long, laborious process that yields a delicious result. Too bad I didn't appreciate the labor or the deliciousness when served lasagna as a 10-year-old. But I ate it under duress and wasn't scarred for life. I love it now. I'd love to eat some of my mom's lasagna tonight. Paging Mary Lee Haywood: "Can I have another chance for lasagna, please?

At supper, Eric and I told Ashton and Alyssa, "You don't have to like it. You just have to eat it." If they didn't finish their supper, that same food made another appearance at breakfast. On rare occasions, we allowed them to make a PB&J sandwich to supplement a meal they didn't like.

We also taught our kids to cook. Kids are more likely to appreciate food they helped prepare.

Takeaway: Your home is not a restaurant. Your kids should eat what you serve. If they don't like what you've cooked, tough. **Benefit to your kids:** They try new foods. They're reminded the world doesn't revolve around them.

Bonus benefit to you: You don't have to be a short-order cook. You won't waste money on takeout when there's a meal already prepared. Following this rule just once will pay for this book.

One-day action plan: At supper tonight, tell your children, "You don't have to like it. You just have to eat it." Don't apologize. If they refuse, save that supper and serve it as the nighttime snack your hungry kids ask for. Then serve any leftovers for breakfast. If you're feeling lenient, allow your children to get by with trying three bites of everything on their plate. Chart your progress here:

One-week action plan: Continue with the one-day action plan. Now, get your children involved in preparing the meals. Give them small, age-appropriate tasks such as washing fruits and vegetables and peeling them with a peeler or even a knife. Chart your progress here:

One-month action plan: Empower your children to plan an entire age-appropriate meal. Take them shopping to buy ingredients. Supervise the cooking. Repeat weekly. Help your child start a list of all the meals he can make. Chart your progress here:

Mealtime
Sometimes I Eat the Last Piece of Cake

"Sometimes I eat the last piece of cake," I told a friend.

Friend's mouth dropped open. In his child-centered world, he served his son. When only one piece of fried chicken, cake, or pie was left, the son got it. That's great for helping the adult parent lose weight. But when a child gets the first and/or the last piece of everything, every single time, he feels entitled. When a parent eats the last piece of cake, a child is reminded that he is not always at the top of the pecking order.

Takeaway: Parents are important. You deserve the best piece and the last piece when you choose to exercise your rights. You earned that cake. Likely, you baked it, or bought it.
Benefit to your kids: They'll learn they're not the most important person in the house all the time.
Bonus benefit to you: Enjoy that chicken, cake, and pie.

One-day action plan: Purposefully take the first or last piece of meat, bread, pie, or cake for yourself at supper in front of your child. Don't apologize. Eat it slowly, enjoying every bite. Write down how you felt and whether your child was shocked:

One-week action plan: Take the last piece of meat, the last piece of bread, the last of the milk, or the last slice of pie at least three times this week. Is it getting easier to be the lady or lord of your castle? Chart your progress here:

One-month action plan: Keep taking the first or last piece when you want it. Sometimes, offer that piece to your child. Be clear that your child should feel grateful, not entitled. Chart your progress here:

Mealtime
Batting or Battling Cleanup

A few years ago, we ate dinner at the home of a dear friend. After we finished eating, her middle-school-aged daughters abandoned their dirty plates and dishes and headed to the computer to play the latest video game. Our friend jumped up and began the drudgery of putting dishes in the dishwasher, putting away food, wiping the table, and sweeping.

Back home on another night, we enjoyed a meal with friends from Trinidad. After we finished, the adults lounged and talked at the table. Ashton and Alyssa jumped up from the table, collected plates and loaded the dishwasher. They found containers for the leftovers, put up the leftover food, and began wiping the counters. As we talked, I handed the broom to Ashton and he began sweeping the floor.

One meal at a time. One chore at a time. That's how my friend, our kids, and I arrived at our supper-time behavior.

I get it. You might find my picture on Wikipedia next to "Control Freak." Putting your child's dishes away yourself is easier than letting them do a suboptimal job. If you send kids off to play and clean up yourself, you don't have to worry about chipped or broken plates. Everything gets done quickly and efficiently. It's easier to find the container you want for the leftover potato salad than to explain which container works best or worse, or tolerate a small amount of potato salad in a huge container.

In the interest of raising independent children, I had to let go of my inner control freak. By age 3, Ashton and Alyssa could toddle to the dishwasher, plate in hand, and shove that plate haphazardly inside. Meanest Daddy, an engineer, often rearranged the plates later after the kids went to bed. Actually, Meanest Daddy often rearranges the dishes I load.

Sure, we lost plates and glasses. Broken plates were a small price to pay. We kept the heirloom dishes packed away and instead invested in heirloom habits that built self-sufficient children.

Takeaway: Cleaning up the kitchen is one of the important life skills your kids need to learn.
Benefit to your kids: They gain confidence when they learn new tasks and become independent.
Bonus benefit to you: You get to relax after meals. You learn to let go of your need to control everything.

One-day action plan: After supper tonight, tell your children to put their own plates, glasses, and silverware into the dishwasher. Do not rearrange the dishwasher while your kids are still in the kitchen. Chart your progress here:

One-week action plan: Now that they've learned to put their own dishes away, tell your children to load your dishes into the dishwasher, too. Ask them to wipe the counters and sweep the floor. Chart your progress here:

One-month action plan: Add putting food away to your children's after-supper chores. Show them where to find the containers. Don't micromanage. Chart your progress here:

Mealtime
Snack Time: The Big Apple

More than 10 years later, my friend Lisa still remembers The Apple I Would Not Waste. We met at a park: Lisa, her two kids, me, Ashton and Alyssa, and two kids I had for a so-called playdate (actually babysitting).

Since I'm tight-fisted, along with being mean, I brought apples as opposed to swinging by a fast-food restaurant. We walked two miles and then stopped by the car for snacks. I handed out the apples all around.

Ashton, Alyssa, and Lisa's kids started munching. The playdate kids stared at me. They stared at the apples. "These apples aren't peeled. These apples aren't cut up," they whined (see page 57). "These apples are what we have," I responded.

The youngest kid took one bite and started walking off to throw his apple away. Meanest Mommy is a runner and is much quicker than a 10-year-old sauntering to a trashcan. "Not so fast," I said. "We don't waste food." He looked back at me in shock, apple in hand over the open trash can. I stared him down. He ate the apple.

My hope is that I scored a lesson about not wasting food, about being polite, and about obeying adults. Yep, that's me, saving the world. One apple at a time.

Takeaway: Allowing children to waste food builds entitled attitudes. Don't let your kids waste food.
Benefit to your kids: Yet another reminder they're not the center of the world.
Bonus benefit to you: You save money on snacks.

One-day action plan: The next time you give your kids a snack or a meal, remind them that your family doesn't waste food, and that they shouldn't take any more food than they can eat. Chart your progress here:

One-week action plan: Whether it's pizza crust, lasagna (see page 82) or a suddenly unwanted apple, don't let your kids dump food they don't want in the trash. Chart your progress here:

One-month action plan: When you're feeling generous, don't make your kids eat the unwanted food right then. Instead, wrap up that food and save it for the next time your children ask for something to eat (see page 83). Chart your progress here:

The Front Porch

If you have more than one child, you've experienced fights. Similar to our stance on parent-to-child negotiations, we rejected negotiating between Ashton and Alyssa (see page 63).

Instead, we had the front porch. Yes, this is the same front porch where Ashton did his thing (see page 46).

When Ashton and Alyssa fought, we sent them to the front porch to work out their disagreement with no parental intervention. We locked all the doors so they couldn't get back in the house until they settled their problems.

One friend told me her parents insisted that she and her sister work out their own agreements on the TV remote and control of the house internet. One sister controlled the remote for 30 minutes starting at the top of the hour. The other took over at half-past. They knew the rules and could negotiate their own exceptions and side agreements.

Caveat: Clearly, if one child is bullying her sibling, an adult needs to step in.

Generally, though, empowering children to solve their own disputes leads to less tattling, less whining (see page 57), and more empowered kids.

Takeaway: Don't sort out your children's disagreements. Empower them to negotiate their own issues.
Benefit to your kids: They learn to solve their own problems. Maybe one of your offspring will become Secretary of State or a hostage negotiator.
Bonus benefit to you: Peace and quiet.

One-day action plan: The next time your children fight, send them to the front porch or another designated area to work out their own problems. Chart your progress here:

One-week action plan: If there's an issue your children continually fight over — the TV remote, taking care of pets, whose turn it is to take out the trash — come up with an equitable, permanent solution, such as one child has control of the remote at the top of the hour and the other gets the remote at half-past. For trash and pets, you can alternate chores for kids for even and odd numbered days or alternate by the week. For more than two children, you can create a chart that works. Chart your progress here:

One-month action plan: Empower your children to suggest their own solution to their common conflicts. Chart their progress here:

Meanest Mommy Travels Light

I love to walk. My whole family loves to walk. We all took a long walk together recently when Ashton was home from Germany and Alyssa was home from seminary.

Rewind 25 years. I remember taking a short walk around my neighborhood with another woman and our babies. She had a gigantic diaper bag stocked with baby food, baby snacks, bottles, diapers, wipes, toys, stuffed animals, tissues, spare stroller wheels, and supplies to build a campfire and an igloo.

I had baby Ashton in a lightweight stroller.

This mom, bless her heart, looked judgmentally at unencumbered me. "What if he gets hungry? What if he gets bored? What if he needs a diaper?" I responded, "We'll do without or go home." As the other woman continued to judge and lecture me, going home sounded more enticing by the minute.

We completed our walk and I didn't have to stop to change a diaper, blow a nose, pull out a selection of toys, fix the stroller, make a campfire, cook a meal, or build an igloo.

Soon, I graduated to carrying Ashton, one diaper, and wipes in a kiddie backpack. I didn't have to worry about curb cuts, steps, or wheels coming off a stroller.

We also wanted our children to graduate quickly from riders to walkers. Although many of his friends rode in strollers until age 6, Ashton graduated to walking on his own two feet before age 4. We had another baby on the way and no plans for a double stroller. We believed in having kids walk on their own two feet as soon as possible and carry their own loads.

When Ashton and Alyssa walked, they didn't get the traveling light concept, literally or figuratively, especially at first. They always wanted to carry a teddy bear, stuffed animal, or other toy. The problem is: kids carrying the item in question always evolves to the mom carrying that item.

My rule was, "You bring the thing, you carry the thing the whole walk. I will not carry it, whatever it is, once you get tired of it." You may remember that rule is how I got promoted from Meanest Mommy in the *World* to Meanest Mommy in the *Universe*!

Ashton and Alyssa learned first to carry their own physical, literal burdens. Working on carrying the non-physical burdens is what raising adults is all about.

Takeaway: You don't always have to be ready to cater to your child's every whim or carry your child's every toy or burden.
Benefit to your kids: Kids learn a lot by doing without, and by carrying their own toys and their own burdens.
Bonus benefit to you: Lighter load. Hands free.

One-day action plan: Next walk, pack light. If your child wants something and you don't have the thing with you, tell him to wait. Chart your progress here:

One-week action plan: Stop carrying toys and other items for your child. Tell her, "If you want it, you carry it." Chart your progress here:

One-month action plan: If your child is age 4 or older and still riding in a stroller, start transitioning her to walking. When she demands, "Carry me," empower her by saying, "You're a big girl now. You can walk." Be sure to have plenty of snuggle time, sitting down. Chart your progress here:

School Days
Empower Your Children to Succeed

Twice in two weeks, I ran into friends with older teens and asked how life was going. Both times, I got some version of this answer, "Busy. There's prom, the SAT, AP tests, projects due…." These women weren't back in high school. They were owning their teenager's problems.

The 17-year-old son of a woman I know decided to ask a girl to his school's spring dance only a few days before the event. Getting a tux, flowers, and dinner reservations became the mom's last-minute problem. Although her friends praised her on social media for being "a good mama," I thought this woman would have been an even better mama if she had empowered her son to handle these last-minute issues.

Another woman I know was canvassing her neighborhood with her high school junior son, asking people if the teen could interview them for a class project. Later, this woman mentioned that her teenager's obligations were the reason she was too busy to pursue her dream of resuming piano lessons.

In all cases, I wanted to say, "Why are *you* busy with *your children's* responsibilities?" Instead, I wrote this chapter and three others on homework, school, and children taking responsibility.

With their constant eating, sleeping, pooping, peeing, burping, and crying, babies are high maintenance. After age 4, most children and teens are as high maintenance as their parents permit. If you've allowed yourself to get in this position, there are ways out.

For homework, when your child is struggling and saying, "I don't get this," listen. But instead of moving quickly to the answer, help your child figure out the problem on his own.

Guide him from what he knows to what he doesn't know. As a piano teacher, I do this all the time. When a student doesn't know a note on the staff or the keyboard, I don't tell her the note. Instead, we work our way from a note the child *does* know, step by step, to the unfamiliar note. Eventually, my piano students internalize the steps of working from the known to the unknown and solving their own problems. If you adopt this practice, then eventually your child also will internalize the process of solving problems by working from the unknown to the known.

Some children take responsibility on their own initiative. An early reader of this book didn't like being nagged by her parents to do her homework in elementary school. So, she made a deal. For two weeks, her parents wouldn't mention homework, tests, or projects. The teacher was in on the plan. At the end of two weeks, this friend scored kudos from her teacher for getting her homework done. At a young age, she broke free of parental management of homework. That was a win for parents and child.

By the time your child is in high school, you should be doing your own thing while he or she completes projects and studies for AP tests. When your teen troubleshoots issues by herself, she becomes smarter and empowered. That makes the next time easier for her, and makes it less likely you'll need to step in.

If you realize you enjoy being needed by your child, stop right now and think about whether you want to go to college, and the first post-college job with your child. Maybe you do want to tag along (see page 117), but I doubt it's practical, smart, or what your child needs.

Remember, we are raising adults, not children.

Takeaway: Don't take on responsibility for your child's homework, projects, and grades.
Benefit to your kids: They learn to be responsible for their own tasks. Empowered people get things done.

Bonus benefit to you: When you stop serving your children and teens, you'll get more done too — whether it's a clean house, a gourmet meal, a girls' night, selling a house, inventing something new, writing a novel, meditating, learning Taekwondo, or earning a college degree or certification for yourself.

One-day action plan: The next time your child says, "I don't get this," while doing his homework, back up to a concept your child does understand and work your way together through the unknown concept. Chart your progress here:

One-week action plan: If your child is middle-school age or older, track how much time you spend helping with homework. Spend less time every day. Chart your progress here:

One-month action plan: When your child has a major project or test coming up, encourage him to chart out a schedule and plan for getting the work done. Chart your progress here:

School Days
Empower Your Children to Fail

After reading the last chapter, you may fear that your children will fail if you follow that advice. Truly, failing early could be the best thing to happen to your child.

When Alyssa was in middle school and early high school, completing and turning in homework was not a high priority for her even though her teachers dinged her with zeros. Eric and I worried and nagged about Alyssa's issue far too much. We worked out the math and told her how many 100s it took to bring a zero up to an A. In case you're wondering, it's 15. The problem got so bad that every time I emailed her teachers on the county schools' Edline program, the subject line of the email auto-completed to "Alyssa zeros."

Finally, we stopped worrying. We stopped nagging. We handed the homework issue to Alyssa where the problem should have remained in the first place. We told Alyssa that her homework was her problem. Her grades were her problem. I'd like to be able to report that Alyssa immediately started turning in all her homework on time. She didn't.

Somehow, despite the zeros, Alyssa did graduate in the top 10 percent of her class. The important issue, though, was that we stopped managing Alyssa's homework and her grades.

Before Alyssa left for college, we told her that if she made bad grades in college, she was coming home and/or paying for the parent share of college bills (see page 117).

In college, Alyssa turned her work in on time. Her class rank at her university was top five. She earned all As in her undergraduate career except for one A-. Her grades and her overall record earned her a place to study at Hebrew University in Jerusalem during the final semester of her undergraduate program. She's now studying for a dual master's degree at Princeton Theological Seminary. We have never emailed or called any of her professors.

I realize you don't want your children to fail. But failing isn't always bad. GE has a culture of "Fail fast. Fail Often. Fail Forward." If the smart folks at GE can learn from failure, so can your child.

Empower your child to make age-appropriate decisions with age-appropriate consequences regarding his education. It's better and cheaper to fail on a homework assignment at age 8 or 12 in elementary or middle school and learn from that mistake as opposed to flunking out of college at age 18, 22, or 28.

Takeaway: Kids need to own their homework and their education. By middle school, your child should take responsibility for his or her homework without endless nagging. If he doesn't do his homework, he should suffer the consequences — that is fail, at school and at home.

Benefit to your kids: Kids learn to take responsibility for their own education and their own failures when the stakes are low.

Bonus benefit to you: Less nagging.

One-day action plan: Tell your middle school or older child you'll remind him just once today to do his homework. After that, it's up to him. Stick to it. Chart your progress here:

One-week action plan: If you've been saying things like "*We* have math homework tonight," stop. Remember, it's your child's homework, not yours. Make that "*Artie* has math homework tonight." If your child is 13 or older, send a note to the teacher to let him know that you're no longer in the nagging business about homework, and that you want your child to learn independence and consequences. Ask the teacher to partner with you. Chart your progress here:

One-month action plan: When the first consequences/failures hit — a zero, C, or even a D or F, instead of an A or B on an assignment or a report card — be strong. Don't take homework back as your problem. Brainstorm with your child for solutions. Offer your child an inexpensive outing with you if she turns in her homework every day for a month with no nagging. Yes, this is a rare exception to the rule you'll hear about: no treats for doing the right thing. Chart your progress here:

School Days
The Exceptions to Not Getting Involved

As you've already seen, I believe strongly in empowering kids to handle their own problems at school. Sometimes, though, a parent must get involved as a fixer.

From an early age, Ashton loved history, especially military history. By 6th grade, he was reading college-level history books about World War I and World War II. His 11th grade AP U.S. History teacher had heard all about Ashton before he got to her class that fall.

The problem was the summer reading assignment. First, Ashton disagreed with the premise of the book, Rachel Carson's *Silent Spring*. We're not going to debate that premise here. Second (building on the first), Ashton didn't read more than a few pages of *Silent Spring*. As you've seen in other chapters, not reading the book wasn't my concern.

Somehow, Ashton managed to write an essay disagreeing with Carson's points without citing anything Carson actually wrote. Ashton's history teacher was rightly disappointed in him.

This history teacher graded Ashton's essay too generously with a C-. Then, based on how angry and disappointed she was, the teacher skewered him on a personal level in her written comments.

The issue was bigger than homework, bigger than grades. Every day in class, the teacher continued to show her disappointment in Ashton, rejecting any attempts he made to contribute to class discussions on other topics. Ashton the history buff started shutting down. I could see two bad years looming because this teacher also taught the next year's class, AP U.S. Government. I envisioned Ashton no longer liking history, or even becoming a troublemaker to live up to this teacher's opinion.

I had to step in. I called the teacher and left a message about the essay. When the teacher returned my call, I could hear the defensiveness in her voice. She was ready for me to argue about his grade.

Instead I said, "I'm not calling about the C. He wrote a crappy (I used another word) essay. He deserved an even lower grade. I'm calling about his relationship with *you*."

This tough, veteran teacher started crying. She knew she had been too hard, personally, on Ashton. I'm not sure what the teacher said to Ashton the next day, but within two days all was well in history-teacher land. Ashton and the teacher got along famously for that year and his senior year in AP U.S. Government. On the afternoon that Ashton graduated from high school, and his teachers became his former teachers, thus eligible for connections on social media, this teacher was his first teacher Facebook friend.

The second issue involved history and Alyssa. She was in the 8th grade and struggling in her history class. Her history grades on her progress reports and report cards were 95-100 but her standardized test benchmark scores (early warning tests before the real tests in the spring) were barely passing. Despite her good grades, Alyssa wasn't learning history. Unlike Ashton, Alyssa was not reading up on history on her own back then. If Alyssa didn't learn history in class, she didn't learn history at all.

After a semester of this non-learning, I went to school. The principal was not available so I talked to the school's testing coordinator. I said, "You're a numbers guy. So here are the numbers. Alyssa is getting grades of 95-100 in class, but scoring poorly on the Standards of Learning benchmark tests. Something's not right."

He responded, "She's still passing the SOL benchmarks. She'll be OK." My response: "I care very little about her SOL test scores and not much more about her grades. What I do care about is that first, she learns history, and second, she likes history. Grades are third and test scores are last place. She needs to be in another class so she can learn history."

The testing coordinator switched Alyssa to a teacher who still cared about teaching, history, and children. Alyssa's grades dropped to Bs at first, but she began learning history. Then, her grades crept back up to As, and this time those grades represented actual learning. Alyssa's standardized test scores — yes, the ones I didn't care about — also went up. Within a year, her original history teacher was assigned to other duties.

If I hadn't gotten involved in these two situations, the consequences could have been dire. Because I didn't have a reputation as a helicopter parent who complained about every issue, I was able to make my voice heard when the situations warranted.

Takeaway: Some battles are truly too big for children, and parents do have to get involved at school. Choose your battles carefully.
Benefit to your child: They get help when they really need help.
Bonus benefit to you: You know you made a difference.

Lifetime action plan: Before stepping in to help your child fight a battle, think hard about whether this battle is one your child should fight on her own. If she truly needs help, then go all out to win.

Going to College with the Kids:
A Cautionary Tale

Alyssa drove six hours up and down the interstate to college by herself. The fall of her senior year, she moved into a house near campus without any parental help. During a semester in Spain, she made all of her own travel arrangements and traveled alone to Poland, England, France, Greece, and Germany. In spring 2019, she spent her final semester in Jerusalem, again managing all the logistics herself.

Alyssa-style independence was the norm a generation or two ago. In the late 1960s, my next-door neighbor drove across country alone to start college. Fifty years later, times have changed — and not for the better — for college students.

One longtime friend of mine drove their young adult (I use the word adult loosely in this case) son to college every day because he refused to learn to drive. She sat outside his classrooms while he was in class and then drove him home at the end of the day. The bus stop for public transportation was a mile or two away — supposedly too far for him to walk. So, the college student's lack of driving skills became a parent problem and disrupted the parent's life for years.

Another friend faced the same situation. For a long time, Grandpa drove his granddaughter to community college at 8 a.m. and picked her up at 2 p.m. after class was done.

With door-to-classroom taxis, the two college students were not motivated to learn to drive.

The game changer for one of those students came when the student's dad began giving her a ride. Dad-as-taxi worked on his schedule, not the kid's schedule. Dad left the house at 6 a.m. and returned home around 6 p.m. That made for a long day for the kid at community college. Suddenly, learning to drive safely and confidently became a priority for the college kid.

I am not advocating pushing a young person who is not ready to get behind the wheel. I am, however, advocating that a lack of driving becomes the young person's issue to deal with — not the parent's problem. Let the young adult budget for the bus, Uber,

Lyft, or find a friend who will take gas money in exchange for a ride.

We live in a college town, and I also have heard from college administrators about parents who check into a nearby hotel the first week of classes to make sure their precious princes and princesses are adjusting to college life.

Some of these parents also come back for a week during mid-terms in the spring to make sure their child is studying. At that point, it's past time to let go.

To these parents, I apologize. I'm sorry I did not write my book sooner.

Managing situations independently builds confidence in children and young adults. In contrast, when you do everything for your kids, you're not helping them. You're preventing your children from becoming strong. Ideally, you'll start when they're young by letting them open their own juice boxes and fix their own plates (see pages 74 and 78).

Your kids need to live their own lives. So do you.

Takeaway: By the time your child is in college, he needs to navigate classes, grades, transportation, moving into a dorm or apartment, and other issues on his own.

Benefit to your kids: They develop the confidence that comes when they solve their own problems.

Bonus benefit to you: More free time and fewer burdens. You'll also save money on a week's hotel stay when your offspring head to college. Or spend that money on a hotel in a place where you can relax and recharge.

One-day action plan: Stop getting involved in your high school or college student's discussions with teachers, professors, future bosses, current bosses, and landlords. Chart your progress here:

One-week action plan: If you are driving your college student to class or to school, empower him to start getting behind the wheel. Take your teen to get his learner's permit if he does not already have it. Then start with moving to the passenger seat as he drives in a parking lot. As soon as he's comfortable behind the wheel, let him drive on the big-boy road. Alternate plan: If your college student is not ready to drive, tell him to brainstorm how he can get to class without your involvement. Chart your progress here:

One-month action plan: When it's time for a new semester, don't take it for granted that you'll help your child move into his room or apartment. Empower him to make the arrangements. Chart your progress here:

Whose Laundry Is It Anyway?
How A One-Time Punishment
Made My Life Easier

I was shocked when I realized the truth. I opened the dirty clothes hampers in my children's rooms and saw clean, folded clothes. Ashton and Alyssa, ages 11 and 7, were too lazy to put their clothes in their dressers. So, they had been putting their clean, folded clothes in their dirty clothes hampers.

I yelled a little bit. Then, I got smart. I told Ashton and Alyssa that for the next two weeks, they were doing their own laundry. I showed them how to operate the washer and dryer. I advised the kids to use cold water only. I told them their clothes would smell better if they didn't leave them in the washer for three days before putting them in the dryer. Then I got out of the laundry business. As it turned out, for good.

After washing and drying their own clothes for two weeks, the kids discovered they liked the responsibility. Children enjoy being able to do things that grownups do, even tasks as simple and boring as laundry. One day, I overheard Ashton bragging to a friend that he knew how to run the washer and dryer. Alyssa was smug, too. She liked knowing she could have clean clothes whenever she wanted.

Ashton ended up with pink socks once and Alyssa shrunk one of her shirts. A few laundry mishaps were well worth the benefit of empowered children.

As for me, no one came to me again, dirty shirt in hand at 6 a.m., insisting that this shirt and only this shirt needed to be clean in time to wear to school. Of the few times they brought laundry home from college, they, not me, washed those clothes. Meantime, I have friends whose college kids still don't know how to use the washer and dryer.

Takeaway: Sometimes the right punishment, such as forcing children to do their own laundry or other household tasks related to the offense, can evolve into a win-win for all concerned.
Benefit to your kids: Children will know how to do laundry and perform basic household tasks.
Bonus benefit to you: Lighter laundry basket. No college kids bringing laundry home for you to wash, dry, and fold.

One-day action plan: If your kids deliberately make a mess or cause a household problem, tie the punishment to their offense. For example, if they track dirt in the house after you asked them to use the doormat, make sweeping their job for the next week. Even if no punishment is involved, show your kids how to move clean clothes from the washer to the dryer and start the dryer. Let them move the next load and start the dryer. Chart your progress here:

One-week action plan: Continue to link punishments to household crimes. But even in the absence of household crimes, show your kids how to put washing soap in the washing machine, switch the machine to cold wash, and start the washer. Let them start the next load. Chart your progress here:

One-month action plan: Empower your children to do their own laundry every time. Chart your progress here:

Church: Meanest Mommy Takes One for the Team

One of my favorite things is playing music in church. When Ashton and Alyssa were 5 and 1, I stepped back from the church piano bench. Otherwise, I risked being the only family member at church.

Playing church music requires the musicians to get to church at least an hour early to rehearse. That meant Meanest Daddy had to get two kids ready by himself, take Alyssa to the church nursery, and then keep 5-year-old Ashton under control during the entire service while I tickled the ivories.

Meanest Daddy is a rocket scientist who helps land spaceships on Mars. But getting two kids ready for church and then wrangling them to behave during the service was harder. Several times

Meanest Daddy said, "Sundays are supposed to be a day of rest, but they're the hardest day of the week for me."

Finally, I heard him. I took a long sabbatical from playing church music and traded the piano bench for the church pew. I found I enjoyed sitting with my family. We tag-teamed giving Ashton the stare of death when necessary. When it was time for Alyssa to graduate from the nursery to big church, Eric and I could play man-to-man defense with Alyssa and Ashton on the family pew.

Now that the kids are grown, I'm playing keyboard and singing at a new church and loving it.

Takeaway: Sure, lead your own life, but know when it's time to be a parent first.
Benefit to your kids: Sane parents, a better marriage, and in our case, church attendance.
Bonus benefit to you: You're juggling fewer balls. When you share the load, your marriage grows stronger.

One-day action plan: Take 10 minutes and think about your volunteer, social, and work commitments. Are any of these commitments preventing you from being the parent you want to be? Write them down and start thinking about whether and how to give something up. Chart your progress here:

One-week action plan: Give something up. Send the email backing out. If it's easier, pause the obligation for six months and then reassess. Chart your progress here:

One-month action plan: Begin spending one-on-one time with each of your children in place of the commitment you let go. Chart your progress here:

Just home from church on Easter. The kids were ready to eat, not take photos.

No TV? No Problem!

Sometimes I forget TV even exists. I have never purchased or owned a television. I have not lived in a house with a TV since the early 1980s. When we got married, Eric and I agreed to try a year of no TV. That year has morphed into decades.

I'm not telling you to get rid of your TV. I hear you. You watch only the History Channel, the news, and science shows. But once you get past withdrawal, limiting television might lead to happier parents and kids.

Children who watch TV and YouTube and are online without any parental control are exposed to a daily diet of violence and sex. They are barraged by constant advertising to buy sugary foods, the latest gimmick, and the latest fad toy.

Tough limits on when, if, and what TV programs are allowed will change your lives. Without a TV on constantly, your children will have more time to read books and play games (see page 157). Settlers of Catan, anyone? Your home will be quieter and calmer. Likely, everyone will get more sleep, too.

Takeaway: Less TV means more family time and more peace.

Benefit to your kids: They get more sleep. They are less likely to ask for something they saw an ad for on TV.

Bonus benefit to you: You get more sleep. Your house is quieter and calmer.

One-day action plan: Unplug the TV for one day. Play family games instead. Chart your progress here:

One-week action plan: Pick two or three days out of the week to go TV-free. Get out of the habit of turning on the TV as soon as you walk into your home or the room(s) with TV(s). Chart your progress here:

One-month action plan: Set a daily TV watching limit, perhaps one hour. Allow yourself one cheat day per week. Go TV-free for one week per month. Chart your progress here:

Getting Clean

Your Kids Don't Have to be the Great Unwashed: Don't Throw in the Towel at Bath Time

Splish splash. I still remember bath time growing up. My siblings and I (Wait, did I give them a chance to vet this chapter? Youngest sibling/ace editor says, "No, you didn't, but we love you anyway.") made mermaids out of our washcloths and swam them around in the tub. We practiced blowing bubbles. We competed for the dirtiest feet. Bath time was fun.

Bath time can be the highlight of your day too, as your child plays with toys, uses bubbles to create a beard and — oh yeah — gets clean. Don't you love the smell of Johnson's baby shampoo?

Not every child gets the memo about bath time being fun. Some children are content to remain the great unwashed. I still remember my mother giving baby Ashton a bath. As she headed to the bathroom with Ashton, Grandma told the rest of us, "A bath relaxes babies."

Soon, we all heard loud wailing from the bathroom. Someone asked, "What's going on?" My dad responded, "Grandma is 'relaxing' Ashton."

Meanest Mommy nearly met her match when she offered to give the Almost Twins a bath. The girls, ages 4 and 5, competed not for the dirtiest feet but for attention. Whining played a major role as in, "Her pulled my haaaiir." (See page 57.)

Fortunately, making bath time a game worked for the Almost Twins. "Simon says … Wash your feet for 10 seconds. Hurry. Fast. OK, done. Now Simon says … Wash your face for 11 seconds."

When Meanest Mommy had to do the washing, she became comfortably dumb. She'd take an arm and say "I'm washing your leg." The Almost Twins first thought Meanest Mommy was nuts. Then they thought bath time was funny. Meantime, they were getting clean and we weren't fighting. Instead of arguing, we had a fun time for free (see pages 147 and 150).

If bath time is a nightly battleground in your home, make it a game. Be willfully stupid. Have fun.

Takeaway: Instead of one more battle, look for ways to make bath time and other conflicts a game.

Benefit to your kids: They're laughing. They're clean, maybe.

Bonus benefit to you: You have fun with your children. You get in the habit of being creative on other parenting challenges.

One-day action plan: Tonight, don't worry about whether your kids get clean. Just make bath time a game. Try Simon Says in the tub. (Simon says wash your arm. Simon says wash your pinkie toe. Wash your leg; Oops! No Simon says!) Chart your progress here:

One-week action plan: If you have more than one child, start a dirtiest feet competition. Add the comfortably dumb game to your repertoire and mix up the body parts you're washing. Chart your progress here:

One-month action plan: Give your kids tickets for two one-hour baths per month. Now you've made bath time special. Chart your progress here:

Getting Clean
If Baths Don't Work, Try Swimming Lessons

Every kid should learn to swim. If they won't take baths, this is another option to get clean. Just kidding. Mostly.

Seriously, Ashton failed toddler swimming lessons three times at our local Recreation Center. Life jackets were a key wardrobe accessory at the beach (see page 52).

We were committed to helping Ashton learn to swim. On the days Ashton didn't have swimming lessons, we went to the Rec Center pool so he could practice swimming. I took him to friends' pools to swim. On vacations, we made it a point to stay in hotels with pools and take time to swim. Still, Ashton wouldn't let go of the pool wall.

Actually, I, too, was a reluctant swimmer who never let go of the wall. I remained in the beginning swimming class at the Charlotte, N.C. YMCA for three years even when taught by the Charlotte Y's formidable, famous, and excellent teacher, Miss Frankie. I was too scared to let go of the wall because even the shallow end of the pool was over my head. I finally learned to swim in a motel pool where the shallow end was only up to my chin.

So, I could relate to Ashton's struggle. I remember the day when — thanks to an insightful, patient teacher in the fourth round of lessons — Ashton finally swam on his own at age 6. Tears flooded my eyes when I saw that little body buoyant in the water, feet kicking, arms dog paddling.

After class, we stopped at Hardee's and ate French fries to celebrate. Yes, sometimes Meanest Mommy is fun and willing to spend money.

A decade later, Ashton had become a strong swimmer. Once, he jumped in a river and saved a struggling child.

Takeaway: Be patient. This is not the time to be mean.
Keep signing kids up for swimming lessons. If the water is over their heads, take them to a shallow pool to learn.
Benefit to your kids: They'll know how to swim, an important life skill.
Bonus benefit to you: While you always have to be vigilant around water, you can worry a little less when your kids are swimmers. You can ditch those life jackets a little sooner.

One-day action plan: Fill the bathtub up as deep you can and let your child try swimming in the tub (see page 132). Chart your progress here:

One-week action plan: Find a pool or baby pool that is not over your child's head. Take him there regularly to practice. Don't obsess over your child's slowness to learn. Chart your progress here, both on the swimming and the not obsessing:

One-month action plan: Keep signing your child up for swimming lessons. Don't be That (over involved) Parent but do talk to the teacher. If one swimming teacher doesn't seem to be a good fit, find another teacher. If you can afford it, consider private or semi-private lessons. Chart your progress here:

We loved our trips to Eleuthera.

Getting Clean
Get a Grip, Get a Shower

"I haven't taken a shower in five days," a friend told me. Was she confessing, complaining, or bragging? I wasn't sure.

Five Days. Without. A Shower. I couldn't fathom it. This mom was not sitting in a hospital vigil at the bedside of a deathly ill child. Just a little busier than usual, with kids ages 5 and 1. So, she set aside her own well-being.

By day five, she felt dirty, smelly, and walked on. Like a doormat, not important, not worth the effort. That's the message she sent to her husband, her children, her friends, and, most of all, to herself.

Personally, I like pounding hot water in the shower waking me up in the morning. I savor soaking in a tub and washing the day's troubles down the drain at night. I enjoy being clean, too. Even a three-minute shower makes a difference.

Takeaway: Having kids does not mean you don't deserve a daily shower. Whether your child is a newborn, a toddler, a tween, or a teen, you can make time for a quick shower or even an occasional bubble bath.

Benefit to your kids: If Mama ain't clean, nobody's happy.
Bonus benefit to you: You're clean, happy, and setting a precedent that you deserve a separate life.

One-day action plan: If you haven't already taken a shower today, head that way now. Secure your child(ren) safely in cribs or playpens. Ignore the screaming and yelling. This first time, a two-minute, military basic training style shower is fine. Chart your progress here:

One-week action plan: Figure out the time of day that works best for a shower. If five minutes of chores don't get done, that's OK. Make your shower a habit. Don't skip more than one day out of seven. Ignore the screaming and yelling. Chart your progress here:

One-month action plan: Look back over four weeks of shower logs. Did the house fall down? Did Social Services take your children? No? Record how you feel. Now add a weekly bubble bath. Chart your progress here:

Going to the Store: No Rewards

Too many children expect a treat such as a toy or candy because their parents went to the store. Or because they behaved with their parents in the store. Or, just because.

As soon as you start rewarding what should be normal good behavior with candy, toys, and other treats, you've set the bar too low. Your reward for this will be children whining for a treat Every Single Trip (see page 57).

We never gave Ashton and Alyssa treats for behaving in a store. The result: They never asked for treats.

What I wish I had thought to do: Reward good behavior with a treat of time together, such as a short game when we got home. A fun time would have further enforced the message that life is about quality time together, not who has the most candy and toys.

Takeaway: Don't reward normal or even excellent behavior with treats.
Benefit to your kids: They learn that good behavior is its own reward.

Bonus benefit to you: More time. More money.

One-day action plan: Reward good behavior with quality time. The next time you go to the store, tell your children before you leave that there will be no treats. Tell them if they behave, you'll play a short game with them when you get back home. Chart your progress here:

One-week action plan: If your children are still asking for treats, tell them that you'll play a longer game if they can go one week without even asking for a treat. Chart your progress here:

One-month action plan: For real growth: If your children are old enough to be trusted, send them on short missions to buy specific items when you take them into small stores. These items should be already on your list and items your kids enjoy such as apples, juice, or their favorite bread. If necessary, bring an empty juice box, juice container, or bread bag so they know exactly what to get. Don't offer a reward, but praise them for success and for being mature. Chart your progress here:

The Pillow Fight and the Puddle

Although I didn't stop practicing piano to play blocks with Ashton that day I mentioned earlier (see page 70), I wasn't serious all the time when Ashton and Alyssa were little. I don't remember how the pillow fight started or how it ended. I just remember 3-year-old Ashton and I bopping each other with pillows.

Bop. Giggle. Bop. Bop. Giggle. Giggle. I forgot about piano practice, homework, supper, and housework. All that mattered that moment was bop, bop, bop, giggle, giggle, giggle with my 3-year-old.

When Meanest Daddy got home, we bopped him, too.

Then there was the puddle.

I was driving home with Ashton and Alyssa and saw the puddle ahead on Ashton's side of the car. I put his window down, sped up, and drove right through the puddle. Ashton got splashed. We all laughed then. We still laugh now.

Years later, Ashton paid me back when he was at the wheel and the puddle was on my side of the car. In fact, every time I ride with Ashton driving and there's a puddle on my side, I brace myself for the splash.

These enduring memories are free.

Takeaway: Be lighthearted and open to opportunities for fun (splashing through puddles in the car or on foot) with your child. For extra credit, try this with your significant other.
Benefit to your kids: Fun times, fond memories, light hearts.
Bonus benefit to you: See benefit to kids.

One-day action plan: Take five minutes to be in the moment with your child doing something easy and free. Chart your progress here:

One-week action plan: Make a reminder to be in the moment. Aim for at least five of these in the moment times with your child in a week. Chart your progress here:

One-month action plan: Look back over the month and meditate or write down how you felt during these fun moments. Think about your relationship with your child: How is it better? Chart your progress here:

No Money? No Problem:
Let the Good Times Roll

As you can see from the bathtub, pillow fight, and puddle stories, you can create lots of fun memories for free. Sadly, many parents feel that spending money equals quality time with their kids.

The AT Mom planned a day out that included a restaurant lunch, a movie, and a museum visit. A day like that with a girlfriend or significant other would be a delight. This plan, however, featured two 5-year-olds. The AT Mom spent at least $50. Therefore, they would have Fun with a capital F.

The first meltdown happened during the restaurant meal. The next meltdown happened at the movie theater. The final stop, the museum visit, was prepaid, but AT Mom and the Almost Twins never arrived at the museum. Instead of fun, another F-word entered the AT mom's mind as she dragged her overstimulated, crying, whining daughters back home.

Sometimes, I did spend money having fun with Ashton and Alyssa. But I never spent a huge amount of money all in one day. If we were out and about, we'd stop at McDonald's and split an ice cream cone three ways. Our cone for three was just enough ice cream to be a treat but not enough to break the bank, spoil supper, or become an expectation. We also learned to share.

We went to museums, but not out to eat and to a movie the same day. Some of our best memories are museum visits gone bad, including the truly horrible IMAX movie *Santa vs. the Snowman*.

For about eight years, we joined a neighborhood pool every summer. Once a summer, and only once, we'd take a fast food picnic to that pool. Total picnic cost for the three of us: about $15.

We enjoyed many free afternoons at local parks — Kiwanis Park, Newport News Park, Waller Mill Park, and York River State Park — for my eastern Virginia readers. We'd walk in the woods, throw rocks in the water, get lost (although Ashton still maintains we were not lost that day at York River State Park), and enjoy the sunshine.

Takeaway: Having fun and spending money don't always correlate. So, have fun. They do grow up fast. But you don't have to break the bank.
Benefit to your kids: They learn fun can be free. Good to know when they're twenty-something and broke.

Bonus benefit to you: Fun times, fond memories, light hearts.

One-day action plan: Take your kids to a local park and let them play for an hour or so. Don't spend any money other than the gas to drive to the park. Chart your progress here:

One-week action plan: Come up with a week's worth of fun, free activities. For a splurge, try splitting a fast food ice cream cone. Chart your progress here:

One-month action plan: Come up with three more weeks of fun, free, or inexpensive activities. Allow yourself one or two events per month that involve spending money but don't spend more than $5 per person. For extra credit, start a money-saving jar and put the money you would have spent in the jar toward a family vacation. Chart your progress here:

Meanest Mommy Gets a Dog

In many families, getting a dog means the lady of the house adds another responsibility. That's great if the lady of the house is the one who wants a dog. Before we got a dog, I made my expectations clear: this new dog would not be my dog. I had enough on my plate. Everyone agreed to that and it stuck.

Our dog, Grommet, has been part of our family for 10 years. We all went together to weekly dog obedience training classes. I do arrange for vet appointments and Grommet often hangs out with me while I write. But Meanest Daddy walks and feeds Grommet daily. Ashton and Alyssa regularly walked Grommet when they lived at home and they still walk him when they visit. They're also game to take him to the vet and buy his food.

Takeaway: Don't get a dog or any pet if you're already overwhelmed with parenting. Don't give in to pleading and get a dog or cat unless a dog or cat is what *you* want.

Benefit to your kids: If you don't get a pet, your children experience the lesson of not getting what they want. If you do get a pet, maybe they'll do a little work and learn to take care of someone besides themselves.

Bonus benefit to you: No pet unless you want the pet.

One-day action plan: If your kids are begging for a cat or dog, tell them you don't want to hear another word about a pet for two weeks. Chart your progress here:

One-week action plan: Continue telling your children to wait two weeks. Tell them the clock restarts if they mention the pet again. Chart your progress here:

One-month action plan: If your children made it through two weeks without mentioning a pet, good for you. Now, lay down the rules that you're prepared to enforce regarding adding a dog or cat to your home. Chart your progress here:

Family Game Night

When Ashton was five and Alyssa a mere toddler, we started Family Game Night. We're not so organized that Family Game Night happens on a set day of the week as it does in some families. But we regularly played games while they were growing up, and we play now when they're home for visits. Their spouses even ask for Family Game Night.

At first, we ran through a lot of the standard children's games, such as Candy Land and Monopoly. Instead of remaining at the Candy Land level, we upped our game. (See what I did there?) We were thrilled to discover Settlers of Catan, a game that plays differently every time. We quickly became enthralled and branched out to other games including Africa, Puerto Rico, Dominion, Tikal, and Ticket to Ride. When we want a simple game, we pick Rummikub.

Early on, we gave Ashton a handicap at Settlers of Catan. When he began reliably winning, we dropped his handicap. Meanest Mommy and Meanest Daddy play to win. Alyssa watched, longing and waiting for the day when she could enter our world and play. After every game, we also made it a point for those who didn't win to say, "It was a good game and I enjoyed it."

What does Family Game Night have to do with being the Meanest Mommy in the Universe? When you're strict with your kids, you need to create shared fun memories too. Family Game Night has given us years of great memories. It's the gift that keeps giving.

Takeaway: Challenging games teach children to aspire to be a part of your world.
Benefit to your kids: They'll learn more and have fun.
Bonus benefit to you: You'll have a good time together playing high-end games that everyone enjoys, instead of struggling not to yawn through yet another silly children's game.

One-day action plan: Tell your children tonight is your first ever Family Game Night. Play a game, any game. Chart your progress here:

One-week action plan: If you're the organized type, set aside one night this week as Family Game Night. Chart your progress here:

One-month action plan: Investigate some of these games to see if they work for your family: Africa, Puerto Rico, Settlers of Catan, Ticket to Ride, Tikal, Dominion, and Rummikub. If you're the organized type, designate one night every week as Family Game Night. Chart your progress and enjoyment here:

The Birthday Party

Many parents spend more money — $200, $300, $500 — on a child's birthday party than on a weekend or week-long adults' getaway at the beach. Of course, many of these parents won't take that beach getaway. I have talked to parents who complain about how broke they are and then describe expensive, elaborate birthday parties that have helped put them in debt.

Even if you can afford an elaborate party, spending several hundred dollars is still too much money and sends the wrong message to children — that they are the center of the universe. Skip the bounce house, clown, pony, and manicures for 6-year-olds.

Ashton's and Alyssa's birthday parties typically involved cake, hotdogs, chips, and maybe a visit to the local pool.

Alyssa's most elaborate party involved three friends, pizza, and an afternoon at our pool. Total spent: about $40. Ashton's most elaborate party was a trip to laser tag with three friends. Total spent: about $100. They appreciated those parties more than if we had planned an elaborate event every year.

The mother of a friend of Alyssa's was even more savvy. This woman typically had birthday parties for her daughter planned around the local public library's free events for children.

Another friend made the rule that she'd plan the party on the even-numbered birthdays with a small to medium budget. On the odd-numbered milestones, the birthday child planned his or her own event within a very tight budget. Her kids learned lifelong lessons about planning and budgeting.

Takeaway: Don't go overboard or in debt for a child's birthday party.
Benefit to your kids: They learn the pleasures of simple gifts. Your kids also learn the value of setting budgets for major events, a good insight to have when they're planning weddings and other celebrations.
Bonus benefit to you: You'll save money. Use your savings to fund an adult getaway.

One-day action plan: Talk to your children about their next birthday and party. Let them know you plan to make some changes. Chart your progress here:

One-week action plan: Tell your children what you have in mind in terms of budget and scale for their next party. Brainstorm ideas. Ask for their opinion. But don't give in to anything you can't afford or don't want to do. Chart your progress here:

One-month action plan: Plan the party with your child and stick to your budget. Chart your progress here:

My Daughter Wants to Read This Book

Alyssa wants to read this book. To me, that is a sign of successful meanest mommy parenting. My daughter is interested not just in herself, or in me as her mother but in me as a separate person. OK, she also wants to know what I've said about her.

Ashton and Alyssa know that while they are very important to me, sometimes other things take priority.

I have an existence apart from them. That's what Mean, Selfish Mommies do. We live our own interesting lives.

Takeaway: Maintain your own separate existence.
Benefit to your kids: They realize you're important, too.
Bonus benefit to you: Respect. (Motown fans, cue up Aretha Franklin.)

One-day action plan: Do something just for you today. Read a few pages of a book, take a walk, take a nap, take a bath, sing, dance, do yoga. Chart your progress here:

One-week action plan: Find time to do something just for you at least five days this week. Also, stop thinking of yourself as Mom with a capital M. Remember you are a wonderful mother but also more than a mother. Chart your progress here:

One-month action plan: Think of a long-range goal just for you, whether it's running a 10k, taking a class, learning a new language, starting a workout program, getting certified to teach, finishing a degree, or learning any new skill. Map out a plan to get there. Chart your progress here:

Alyssa and I had epic adventures in Spain.
This photo was after Mass in Córdoba.

Out of the nest but still in our lives. We went to France in May 2018: Battlefields, croissants, and swimming in the chilly English Channel.

We're Almost Done!

One day, your children will leave your house. At least, they should. When they do, crying is normal. Not having a life, though, is inexcusable. If you've been taking the advice in this book, you'll have free time, a little extra money, and a life with some or all of the following or something else that brings you joy: a career, a side job, volunteer gigs, hobbies, friends, running, hiking, dancing or CrossFit. If you didn't do the action plans in each chapter, go back and do them now.

More Resources

If you want to know more, please check out my website, themmitu.com. Here, you'll find my blog, action plans for download (password: meanestmommyrocks), questions from readers answered, opportunities to sign up for coaching, and my (coming soon) podcast.

I welcome emails from readers: mmitu@themmitu.com

About Me: I'm a writer who covers cool technology, careers, education, personal finance, and health. I also teach piano. I play piano and sing jazz, rock, and country. I run half-marathons. I kayak all year long, as long as the water's smooth. I am happily married for 30-plus years to the love of my life, Eric Queen. We love our empty-nester, TV-free life in Williamsburg, Virginia. I play on the praise team at my church, Stone House Presbyterian, where I'm also an elder. We are close to Ashton and his wife, Amanda, and Alyssa and her husband, Frederic. In fact, we enjoy their company.

Author photo by Kimberly Kiely.

In the summer of 2022, we had a wedding (Ashton and Amanda) and a wedding celebration (Alyssa and Frederic) in six days! Left to right: Ashton Queen, Amanda Queen, Frederic Mitchell, Alyssa Mitchell, Karen Queen, Eric Queen.

Photo credit: Caleb Timmerman.